Buddha Book
A Meeting of Images

Buddha Book
A Meeting of Images

by **FRANK OLINSKY**   In association with **TRICYCLE BOOKS**

Introduction by ROBERT A. F. THURMAN

CHRONICLE BOOKS

SAN FRANCISCO

ACKNOWLEDGEMENTS

Buddha taught that everything is interdependent. With that in mind I would like to express my gratitude to the following people who were involved with the creation of this book from its formless state to that which you now hold in your hands: Helen Tworkov, Lorraine Kisly and the past and present staff of *Tricycle: The Buddhist Review*—especially Carole Tonkinson for her encouragement and Philip Ryan for his extensive behind the scenes efforts; Kim Witherspoon (and her) Associates for finding *Buddha Book* the perfect home; Nion McEvoy, Christina Wilson, Pamela Geismar and everyone at Chronicle Books; Bob and Nena Thurman; all the contributing artists and photographers, galleries, museums, representatives and agencies. Thanks also to everyone who presented Buddha images that were for whatever reason not included. Special thanks to Terry Allen, David Byrne, Lynn Davis, Diane Dubler, Alex Grey, Mayumi Oda, John Bigelow Taylor and Nitin Vadukul for their kindness and generosity. Deepest thanks and love to Georgia Willett for her continued support, assistance, and baked goods.

Library of Congress Cataloging-in-Publication Data available.

ISBN: 0-8118-1777-6

Designed by Frank Olinsky
Printed in Korea

Distributed in Canada by Raincoast Books
8680 Cambie Street
Vancouver, British Columbia V6P 6M9

10 9 8 7 6 5 4 3 2

Chronicle Books
85 Second Street
San Francisco, California 94105

Web Site: www.chronbooks.com

For My Teachers

THE FOUR IMMEASURABLES

May all beings have happiness and the causes of happiness;

May all beings be free from suffering and the causes of suffering;

May all beings never be separated from the happiness free from suffering;

May all beings have equanimity, free from attachment and aversion.

Baby Buddha
From the film *Little Buddha*
by Bernardo Bertolucci
1993
India

When I look at images of the Buddha I am reminded that it is said that we all possess Buddha-nature, the potential to become a Buddha, and somehow things seem to come into better focus. I can't really explain why. Perhaps it has something to do with there being what some teachers, Gurdjieff among others, have called objective art. According to this theory, there are certain forms that embody higher consciousness and can transmit this awareness to others by their mere presence. They are time capsules of awareness.

I once had the experience of wandering through the Metropolitan Museum of Art when all of a sudden I sensed a strong presence in a room I was passing through. I looked around, but there were no people, only some old Chinese Buddhist statues. One figure in particular seemed to be the source of this "presence"—a large ceramic lohan (holy one or saint). I was so overwhelmed that I had to sit down. I didn't share this experience with anyone—and no, I wasn't on drugs. A short while after this I read an article by a Buddhist teacher who talked about the phenomenon of certain statues having the effect I had experienced. Accompanying this article was a photo of the very same lohan.

Buddha Book is an extension of the aesthetic vision I brought to *Tricycle: The Buddhist Review* as its original art director and, later on, its cover designer and creative consultant. *Tricycle* has been a popular voice of Buddhism in America for over five years. It has presented Buddhism and related topics from a perspective of both respect and inquiry. This might seem like a contradiction, but it is actually in keeping with the Buddha's teachings. He taught that one should only accept things based on personal experience and analysis, not blind faith. He further stated that this approach was to be applied even to his teachings. I believe this attitude is a key to the magazine's success.

Buddhism has changed throughout history as it migrated from India into the various countries of the East. The outward forms, practices, and rituals adapted to reflect each culture. The growth of Buddhism in the West is no exception. As more Americans become influenced by Buddhism, so has Buddhism been affected by American culture. Buddhist terms like *karma* and *zen* are household words, and shaved-headed monks populate commercials for soft drinks and laptop computers. Monks chant at rock concerts, and there are many web sites devoted to Buddhist teachings.

Buddhism has the reputation of being only about life's suffering. This is not the whole story. During *Tricycle* editorial meetings I have encouraged a sense of humor. As the Vietnamese Zen Master Thich Nhat Hanh has said, "Suffering is not enough." Why else would the Dalai Lama have such an amazing laugh?

It is with this spirit I have collected Buddha images ranging from the funky to the sublime. There are traditional masterpieces and works by contemporary artists. Each image seems to have things to say. As you look at them, also "listen deeply" and, most importantly, enjoy yourself.

FRANK OLINSKY
January, 1997

INTRODUCTION
by ROBERT A. F. THURMAN

Footprints of the Buddha, Devotional Shrine
Tamara W. Hill, photographer
1972
Mahabodhi Temple
Bodhgaya, India

The Image of the Buddha

A Buddha is an archetype understood by most Buddhists as an ideal pattern toward which a conscious being directs his or her evolutionary striving. "Buddha" is glossed by commentators at least as early as the Indian philosopher Yashomitra (fifth century CE) as "awakened" (*vibuddha*) and "full-bloomed" or "perfected" (*prabuddha*)—awakened from the sleep of misknowledge and perfected in both the wisdom that knows reality precisely and the universal compassion that accomplishes the goals of all living beings.

Thus Buddhas are the culmination of beings' development through long experience in lesser forms like the human and the divine. If the goal of all beings is perfect happiness, and if beings are too naturally sensitive to others to be perfectly happy unless others are also perfectly happy, then a Buddha is the form of life that experiences perfect happiness within itself while feeling simultaneously fully connected to the perfect happiness of all other beings. That is why a Buddha is transhuman, an evolutionary mutation from the human species—a glorious butterfly emerged from a drab human cocoon. Such a perfect being—finite yet infinite, present yet timeless, perfectly happy yet perfectly aware—is almost inconceivable in normal human terms. Buddhist art attempts to convey this inconceivable life form to humans, gods, and other animals by imaginative and artistic means.

Buddhas have all once been human, and they have been every conceivable form of animal, in every conceivable realm of the hells, the earth, and the heavens, in one previous life or another. They retain the human form to emphasize the connection with humanity, in order to teach and to encourage humans to strive to become Buddhas themselves. "Buddha" is thus not the personal name of a particular human or divine being, and there are infinite possible Buddhas inspiring beings in infinite other worlds as well as here.

On a level often esoteric for humans, a Buddha also constantly manifests divine forms of various kinds in order to communicate with the gods. Most Buddhists are not at all atheistic and believe in the existence of many gods. Buddhas are intimately acquainted with all the gods and have reported that they have not yet encountered one who is absolutely omnipotent or responsible for the creation of the infinite universe in its limitless variety.

The Buddha of this world in this era is Shakyamuni, born around 563 BCE in northern India. A large literature of Life Stories (*Jataka*) give specific details of previous lives of our Buddha when he was a *bodhisattva*, or 'enlightenment hero,' a being on the way to buddhahood. We call him "our Buddha" since he manifested in the full-fledged Buddha form in our recent history and continues to impact our lives more than twenty-five hundred years later.

There are many groups of Buddhists in our world of course, each of which sees the Buddha in its own way. Thus, we note that Buddha images created in particular Buddhist nations tend to portray his body in a form similar to their own particular physiognomy. And there is a variety of kinds of Buddha images, just as there is a variety of

Buddha life stories, ranging from more humanized to more divinized views of him—or her, as there are a few, more rare, female Buddha forms.

The Buddhists of Sri Lanka, Burma, Thailand, and Cambodia have inherited the Theravada form of what some scholars call Early, even Original, Buddhism, which I prefer to call Monastic, or Individual Vehicle, Buddhism, in which the Buddha is much concerned with the liberation of individuals through their reeducation in a monastic community. They see the Buddha in a somewhat humanized way and consider there to be very few other Buddhas. Still, their "humanized" Buddha is far from what a modern secular humanist would think of as human. He is considered to be the result of deeds performed in thousands of former lives and he performs numerous miracles in this life. He converses with the gods, travels to various heavens, flies through the air, multiplies his body immeasurably, has clairvoyance, clairaudience, telepathic and telekinetic powers, and so forth—even the relics of his body have enormous magical properties. The Buddha's "human" form is highly abnormal, with a freakishly domed cranium, long ears, webbed fingers and toes, and numerous other auspicious signs on his body. The point is, even these Monastic Buddhists consider the Buddha to have evolved into a culminatory life-form distinct from ordinary human beings. In fact, according to much evidence, these Buddhists were originally so awed by the Buddha's presence and memory that for generations they did not dare to portray his image, representing his presence by a symbol such as a royal wheel, a Bodhi tree, or a footprint.

In the schools of Buddhism of India of the first millennium CE and of East Asia, China, Korea, Japan, and Vietnam, the Buddha is understood as a life form verging into the divine. These are the schools of Messianic, or Universal Vehicle, Buddhism, which first emerged in India around 100 BCE and discovered or created a whole new collection of scriptures that portray the Buddha in a new light. In these Universal Vehicle scriptures, the Buddha is determined to liberate the whole of society, and even all sentient beings in the universe. His activity as a bodhisattva was now depicted on a much vaster canvas. The miraculous performances and bodily forms he used for teaching people were expanded to cosmic proportions, and he also manifested himself in celestial Buddha forms like the Buddha Amitayus (Immeasurable Life) of the Western Pure Land, Sukhavati; Bhaishajyaguru, the dark blue Medicine Buddha; Vairocana, the cosmic Buddha of the galaxy; and Akshobhya, the Buddha of the Eastern Pure Land, Abhirati.

A formal theory of buddhahood was elaborated, the theory of the three bodies of a Buddha. All Buddhas are presented as having a truth body, an infinite presence in unity with the absolute infinite reality of everything and every being, a body shared by all Buddhas. This truth body is indivisible from the numerous beatific and emanation bodies, which are the embodiment of the perfected evolutionary streams of the individual Buddhas' numberless previous lives. The beatific body of each Buddha is ineffable, formed of pure light invisible to ordinary humans and gods, a state in which each enjoys full realization of oneness with the infinite. Out of its bliss this beatific body spontaneously generates emanation bodies, manifestations that can be perceived by ordinary beings and that can educate them in the possibility of their own attainment of buddhahood, can help them evolve, and can impart liberating instructions to them. The emanation bodies are categorized into three types: supreme emanation body, living emanation body, and art emanation body. The supreme emanations are Buddhas like Shakyamuni, replete with the hundred and twelve marks of a superbeing, who occur in a world only when a great number of beings are ripe for liberation. The living emanations are the numerous ordinary-seeming beings who yet accomplish the Buddha work of teaching, developing, and liberating beings. And the art emanations are all of the artistic representations of the Buddha, including sculptural images, paintings, books, and modern media like film and video, as well as the artists who create them, as long as they are working with pure motivation.

A third vehicle of Buddhism, known as the Apocalyptic, Diamond, or Tantric Vehicle, developed in India in the fifth to twelfth centuries CE and spread to India, Tibet, Mongolia, and Japan. In the Tantric Vehicle the apocalyptic, time-collapsing dimensions of buddhahood were revealed, and Buddhas were understood even more as omnipresent and magically active in developing all beings on the planet, manifesting infinite forms in micro- and macrocosmic dimensions. The universe is presented as literally crawling with Buddhas. The fortunate individuals who become aware of this gain access to their own Buddha potential and actuality through the gateway of Tantric initiation. They then enter into mandala-palace universes and subtle virtual-reality dimensions that expand out of the dynamic experiences sometimes briefly glimpsed in the extreme zones of dream realms, sexual orgasm, and death. The forms the Buddhas manifest in these dimensions often have multiple heads, arms, and legs; they adopt divine forms that visually reflect the inconceivable nature of their realizations and capabilities. These are the Tantric archetype deities for which Tibetan art has become so justly famous.

To realize how an ordinary Buddhist in ancient times might have understood the evolutionary transformation of the Buddha form, it helps to listen to Nagarjuna, the great Indian philosopher and yogin of the early centuries CE. He writes to his friend the South Indian king Udayibhadra:

> O great King, listen to how your body will be adorned with the . . . signs of a great being. From your proper honoring of stupas, worthies, holy persons, and the elderly, you will become a universal monarch, your hands and feet marked with wheels. O King, always maintain firmly your vows to practice; you will then become a bodhisattva with very level feet. From your gifts and pleasant speech, purposeful and harmonious behavior, you will have hands with glorious fingers joined by webs of light. . . . From your never doing harm and freeing the condemned, your body will be beautiful, straight and large, tall with long fingers and broad backs of the heels. . . . From your reconciling in peace friends who have been opposed, your glorious private organ will retract into a sheath of skin [like a stallion]. . . . By striving to practice what you preach, your crown dome will stand out prominently,

symmetrical as a banyan tree. From your speaking true words gently over the years, your tongue will be long and your voice like Brahma's. From your always being honest, you will have lion cheeks, glorious and invincible. From your respecting and serving others and following your duty, your teeth will shine, white and even. From your peacemaking speech, steady and soothing, you will have forty glorious teeth, evenly spaced and effective. Through viewing things with love, free of lust, hate, and delusion, your eyes will be bright and blue, with eyelashes like a bull.

(Nagarjuna, *Precious Garland*, trans. P. J. Hopkins, London: Allen & Unwin, 1975, pp. 43–45)

Nagarjuna reminds the king that these marks of a superbeing as achieved by a universal monarch are like a firefly in the sun compared to the same characteristics as achieved by a perfect Buddha, who evolves out of inconceivably greater merit and wisdom. He concludes by saying that the causes of an emanation body of a Buddha are immeasurable.

To come back to the beginning of this essay, we can now see how Buddhists regard the Buddha form as an archetype, a pattern encoding the fruition of an amazing process of evolution. The Buddha form of Shakyamuni serves to remind us of what one human being did become, through eons of acts of generosity, justice, tolerance, and enterprise, and profound attainments of concentration, wisdom, arts, prayer, power, and intuition. This then can inspire us to dedicate our efforts to become just like that ourselves, to find truly satisfying happiness, and to bring along with us all those others whom we love.

The Monastic Vehicle scriptures formally disclaim any compulsion for the practitioner to emulate the Buddha's evolutionary career, and they have no explicit teaching of an evolutionary development through compassion. They show in the Life Stories (*Jataka*) how a being reaches evolutionary perfection over countless lives through acts of generosity, self-sacrifice, and self-transcendence. Art produced in Monastic Vehicle traditions depicts a human-looking Shakyamuni Buddha seated in meditation, standing still with a hand raised in a gesture of teaching, or lying on his side at his time of death, or entry into nirvana. Scenes from the *Jataka* stories show him in acts of mercy and wisdom in previous human and noble animal lives.

The Universal Vehicle scriptures state bluntly that it is impossible to attain buddhahood while remaining embedded within a coarse human body lacking the hundred and twelve signs of superhuman evolutionary perfection. This surprises us because we may think of "enlightenment" primarily as a mental event. We must try to conceive of enlightenment as physically evolutionary as well as mentally transformative, the perfect embodiment of compassion as well as the perfect realization of wisdom. Images from the schools of Universal Vehicle Buddhism show godlike, haloed Buddhas, often surrounded by handsome and richly adorned bodhisattvas and hosts of lesser deities and seekers.

In the Tantric Vehicle the exceptionally intrepid person, under the irresistible pressure of overwhelming compassion for suffering beings, can accelerate this immense transformatory process into just one or a few lifetimes of intense effort. The adept learns to enter the subtle dimension of virtual reality where time and space can be compressed, and while within that dreamlike realm accelerates the evolutionary mutational process to an unimaginable degree. Art of the Tantric Vehicle presents Buddhas in highly charged situations—in ecstatic union or triumphing over demonic opponents—as well as preaching to multitudes of beings both humble and exalted.

Underlying the variations among Buddhist traditions is a unity of inspiration and aspiration. The Buddha image serves as a refuge, a beacon, and a template for creativity. Buddha images are Buddhas themselves in a very real sense—as art emanation bodies—because they have the power to transform.

This book of illustrations of the Buddha image, informal and abstract as well as formal and figurative, chosen by a Western Buddhist artist for a general Western audience, provides a gateway through which to glimpse the jewel of the possibility of evolutionary perfection. It is not necessary to understand all the Buddhology of the various Buddhist civilizations to enjoy them. The purpose of the Buddha form is to produce happiness in those who encounter it, so all the viewer need do is enjoy these sublime images of beauty.

Loshan Buddha
John Bigelow Taylor,
photographer
1981
Near Chengdu, China

Shrine to the Buddha
Tamara W. Hill, photographer
1972
Mahabodhi Temple
Bodhgaya, India

Large Buddha (Little Man)
Photographer, date,
and location unknown

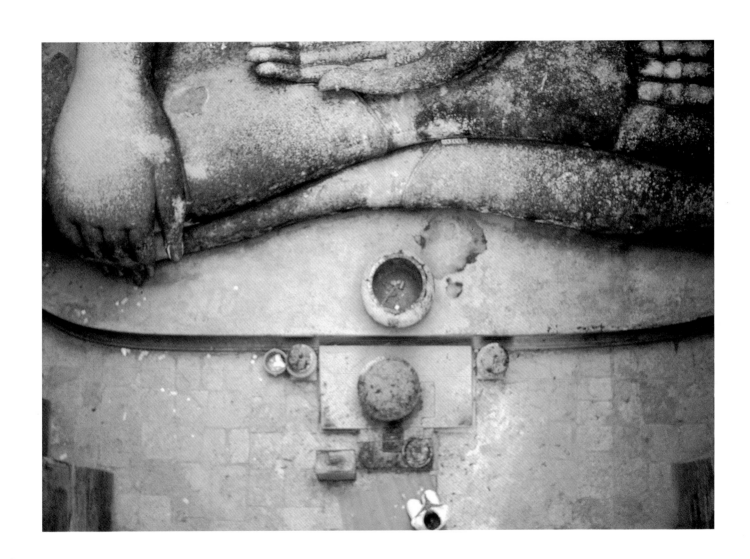

Seated Buddha
Brenda Holoboff,
photographer
Near Takahashi
Okayama-ken, Japan

Buddha in Banyan Tree
Bobby Neel Adams,
photographer
Sukhothai, Thailand

Buddha Head
Cynthia Abbott, photographer
Myanmar (Burma)
Bronze

Buddha Head
Michael Tong, sculptor
Sally Boon, photographer
Socrates Sculpture Park
Queens, New York
Steel

Trouble in Paradise
Terry Allen
1996
Pastel on paper

Homeless Buddha
Izhar Patkin/Nam June Paik
1993
Painted and silkscreened canvas on wood structure,
neon, found objects, 3 Samsung 13" TV sets,
1 Sony laser disc player, 1 original Paik laser disc

Vairocana Series
Douglas Winiarski, photographer
1992
Chuang Yen Monastery
Carmel, New York

Baby Buddhas outside Temple
David Byrne, photographer
1991
South India

Buddha with Children
Patrick Loughran, photographer
Japan

Putt Putt Buddha (15th Hole)
Jim Crump, photographer
1995
Biloxi, Mississippi

Yakushi Nyorai
Enku
circa 1675–1695
("mature period")
Japan
Wood

Buddha
Mayumi Oda
Drawing

Seated Buddhas
Marcia Lippman, photographer
Ayutthaya, Thailand
Sepia-toned photograph

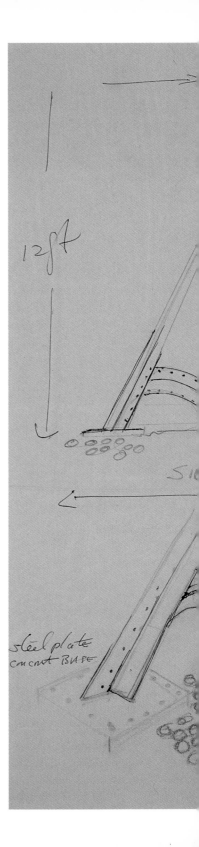

Meditation
Mac Adams
1996
Strasbourg, France
Metal and stone, preliminary drawing

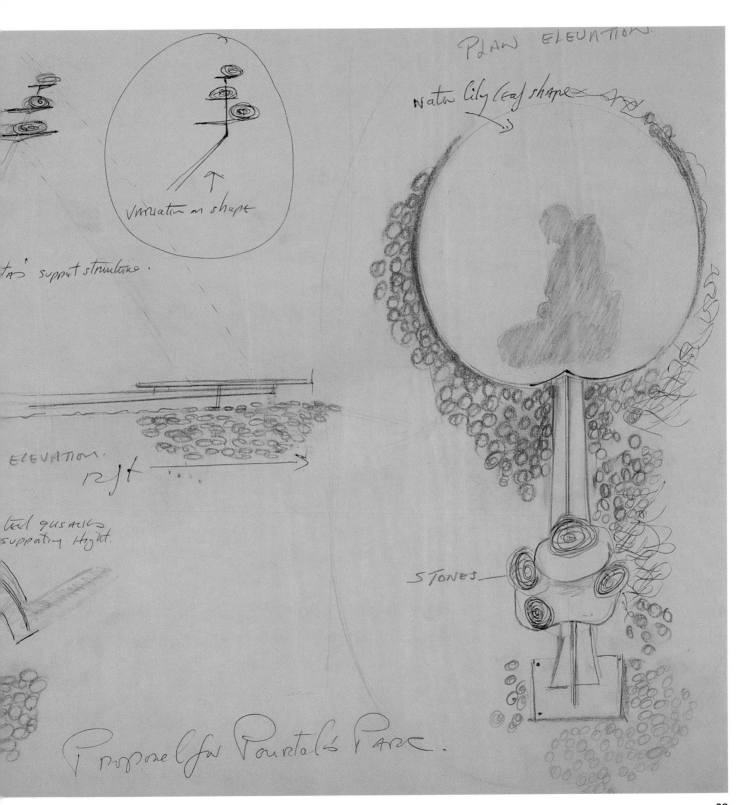

PLAN ELEVATION.

Water lily leaf shape

variation on shape

support structure.

ELEVATION right

steel armature supporting flight.

STONES

Proposed for Pourtalés Park.

Buddha Drawing
Allen Ginsberg
1991
Ink on paper

Allen Ginsberg 4/9/91   New York City.

40

Monk Scaling Unfinished Buddha
Neil Farrin, photographer
Wat Saton Kangthon, Thailand

Back of Buddha
Patrick Loughran, photographer
Japan

Gold Buddha
David Byrne, photographer
Myanmar (Burma)

The Blue Hole
Terry Allen
1986
Mixed media

Stupa
Dean Chamberlain,
photographer
1996
Sante Fe, New Mexico

Medicine Buddha
1635–1705
Tibet
Paint on fabric

Anaradhapura
Nancy Shanahan, photographer
1986
Ruvanvelisaya Dagoba
Sri Lanka

Buddha
Jack Kerouac
1956–1960
Painting

Buddha
Mayumi Oda
Ink on paper

following page:
**Shakyamuni Buddha
with Two Disciples
and the Eighteen Arhats**
John Bigelow Taylor,
photographer
Mid-15th century
Central Regions, Tibet;
probably Tsang
Tangka; gouache on cotton

53

Untitled
Rudolf Stingel
1994
Cast urethane rubber

Shakyamuni Buddha
John Bigelow Taylor,
photographer
Mid 11th to 12th century
Western Tibet
Brass, with traces of
blue pigment in the hair;
sealed with relics inside

Statue of the Buddha
Nancy Shanahan, photographer
1983
Mahabodhi Temple
Bodhgaya, India

Po Lin Buddha
Jake Wyman, photographer
Lantau Island, Hong Kong

Buddha
Lynn Davis, photographer
1993
Sukhothai, Thailand

Buddha
Lynn Davis, photographer
1993
Sukhothai, Thailand

Giant Buddha
John Bigelow Taylor,
photographer
1972
Bamiyan, Hindu Kush
Afghanistan

Loshan Buddha
John Bigelow Taylor, photographer
1981
Near Chengdu, China

Loshan Buddha
John Bigelow Taylor, photographer
1981
Near Chengdu, China

In the Between: Fleeting Head
Arlene Shechet
1994
Hydrocal paintskins, steel, concrete

Buddha Statue
Nancy Shanahan, photographer
1986
Tikse Gompa (monastery)
Near Leh, Ladakh, India

Bodhnath Stupa
Nancy Shanahan,
photographer
1983
Kathmandu Valley, Nepal

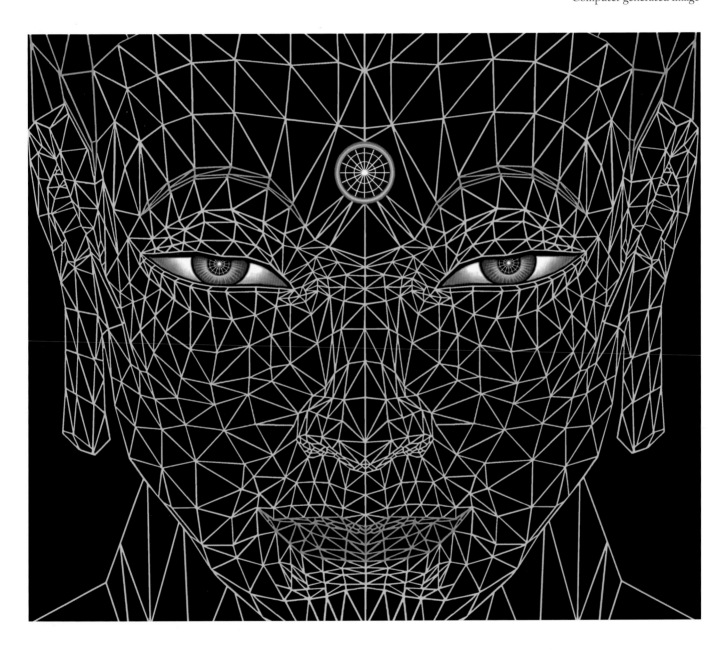

Stone Buddha Head
John Bigelow Taylor, photographer
6th century, Chi Dynasty
Shan Dong Province, China

Tête (Le Bouddha)
Henri Matisse
1939
Charcoal on paper

**Reclining Buddha
at Shwethalyaung**
Nancy Shanahan, photographer
1986
Pegu, Myanmar (Burma)

Sleeping Buddha
Bobby Neel Adams, photographer
Ayuthya, Thailand

Bedrock Buddha
Linda Connor, photographer
1979
Sri Lanka

Sleeping Buddha (1 year later)
Bobby Neel Adams, photographer
Ayuthya, Thailand

Reclining Buddha
Michael Freeman, photographer
Wat Xieng Khwan
Near Vientiane, Laos

Monk Reading Newspaper
Bruno Barbey, photographer
1977
Smaller Shwedagon Temples
Yangon (Rangoon)
Myanmar (Burma)

Fasting Buddha Statue
Nancy Shanahan, photographer
1986
Lahore Museum
Peshawar, Pakistan

Emaciated, Fasting Buddha
Cynthia Abbott, photographer
Myanmar (Burma)

**Reclining Buddha
with remains of
Khmer Rouge victims**
Philip Jones Griffiths,
photographer
1980
Sisophon, Cambodia

Starving Buddha
Bobby Neel Adams,
photographer
Near Chaingmai, Thailand

One Thousand Bodhisattvas
Enku
circa 1675-1695 ("mature period")
Japan
Wood

The Thousands
Anjali Jacques Oulé, photographer

Wax Peace Buddhas
Artist unknown
Ellen Danenhower Colyer, photographer
1996
Vondel Park
Amsterdam, Netherlands

Buddhafield
Frank Olinsky
1994
Computer illustration

Cave of the Thousand Buddhas
Gupta period, 5th century CE
Cave No. 2, Ajanta Caves
Maharashtra, India

Buddhas
Marcia Lippman, photographer
Shwedagon Pagoda
Yangon (Rangoon), Myanmar (Burma)
Hand-tinted, sepia-toned
photograph

Still Time Series
Arlene Shechet
1993–1994
Hydrocal, acrylic paint, wood stools

Seated Buddha
c. 11th century
West Tibet, Ladakh
Wood, with gold and pigments

**Painted Stone Buddha
on Steps to
Swayambunath Stupa**
Nancy Shanahan, photographer
1983
Kathmandu Valley, Nepal

**Shakyamuni Buddha
in Vajrasana**
John Bigelow Taylor,
photographer
Before 1227
Khara Khoto, Central Asia
Tangka; gouache on cotton

previous page:
Psychedelic Buddha
Erika Alonso
1996
Computer illustration
from traditional tangka

**Shakyamuni Buddha
Attaining Parinirvana**
John Bigelow Taylor, photographer
Late 19th–20th century
Central Regions, Tibet,
or Eastern Tibet
Tangka; gouache on cotton

CREDITS

Hardcover photographs: © Lynn Davis. Courtesy of Houk Friedman Gallery

7 Courtesy of Bobby Neel Adams

8 Courtesy of Miramax Films and Recorded Picture Company, Ltd.
Video photography courtesy of Nitin Vadukul

10 © Tamara W. Hill

16 © John Bigelow Taylor

17 © Tamara W. Hill

18 Collection of Ann Shaftel MA, MSc Conservator of Thangkas

19 © 1986 Nancy Shanahan

20 Courtesy of Brenda Holoboff

21 Courtesy of Bobby Neel Adams

22 Courtesy of Cynthia Abbott

23 Courtesy of Sally Boon

24-25 © Terry Allen, 1996. Collection of Mr. & Mrs. Roy H. Cullen

26 Courtesy of Izhar Patkin/Nam June Paik and Carl Solway Gallery
Photograph by Chris Gomien

27 Courtesy of Bobby Neel Adams

28-29 Courtesy of Douglas Winiarski

30-31 Courtesy of Todo Mundo, Ltd.

32 Courtesy of Patrick Loughran

33 Courtesy of Jim Crump

34 Courtesy of Kazuaki Tanahashi. Photograph by Tetsuo Kurihara

35 Courtesy of Mayumi Oda and Parallax Press

36-37 Courtesy of Marcia Lippman

38-39 Courtesy of Mac Adams.
Photography by Mac Adams and Klaus Stöber

40 © Allen Ginsberg. Courtesy of Frank Olinsky

41 Courtesy of Jon Kaplan

42 Courtesy of Patrick Loughran

43 Courtesy of Neil Farrin/Profile Photo Library

44 Courtesy of Todo Mundo, Ltd.

45 Courtesy of Todo Mundo, Ltd.

46 Courtesy of Hedy Klineman and Bridgewater/Lustberg Gallery, NYC

47 © Terry Allen, 1986

48 © Dean Chamberlain

49 From *Tibetan Medical Paintings.* © Serindia Publications 1992

50 © 1986 Nancy Shanahan

51 © John Sampas. The Estate of Jack and Stella Kerouac
Photograph by John Suitor

52 Courtesy of Mayumi Oda

53 © John Bigelow Taylor

54 Private collection, New York. Courtesy of Paula Cooper Gallery

55 © John Bigelow Taylor

56 © 1987 Nancy Shanahan

57 Courtesy of Bobby Neel Adams

58 © D. Jake Wyman

59 Courtesy of Nam June Paik and Holly Soloman Gallery

60 © Lynn Davis. Courtesy of Houk Friedman Gallery

61 © Lynn Davis. Courtesy of Houk Friedman Gallery

62 © Lynn Davis. Courtesy of Houk Friedman Gallery

63 © John Bigelow Taylor

64-65 © John Bigelow Taylor

66 © John Bigelow Taylor

67 Courtesy of Donald L. Sanders and John Bigelow Taylor/Diane Dubler

68 Courtesy of Arlene Shechet

69 © 1986 Nancy Shanahan

70 © 1983 Nancy Shanahan

71 Courtesy of Alex Grey

72 Collection: Arnold Lieberman. Photograph © John Bigelow Taylor

73 © 1997 Succession H. Matisse, Paris/Artist Rights Society (ARS), New York

74 Top: © 1986 Nancy Shanahan
Bottom: Courtesy of Bobby Neel Adams

75 Top: Courtesy of Linda Connor
Bottom: Courtesy of Bobby Neel Adams

76 Courtesy of Michael Freeman

77 Courtesy of Bruno Barbey/Magnum Photos, Inc.

78 © 1986 Nancy Shanahan

78-79 Courtesy of Cynthia Abbott

80-81 Courtesy of Philip Jones Griffiths/Magnum Photos, Inc.

81 Courtesy of Bobby Neel Adams

82 Courtesy of Kazuaki Tanahashi. Photograph by Tetsuo Kurihara

83 © 1986 Nancy Shanahan

84 Courtesy of Anjali Jacques Oulé

85 Courtesy of Ellen Danenhower Colyer

86 © Frank Olinsky

87 Courtesy of Kazuaki Tanahashi. Photograph by Tetsuo Kurihara

88 Scala/Art Resource, NY

89 Courtesy of Marcia Lippman

90 Courtesy of Arlene Shechet

91 © The Cleveland Museum of Art,
Andrew R. and Martha Holden Jennings Fund

92 © 1983 Nancy Shanahan

93 © John Bigelow Taylor

94 Courtesy of Erika Alonso

95 © John Bigelow Taylor